Part 1

Animals in Flowers

Test your colors

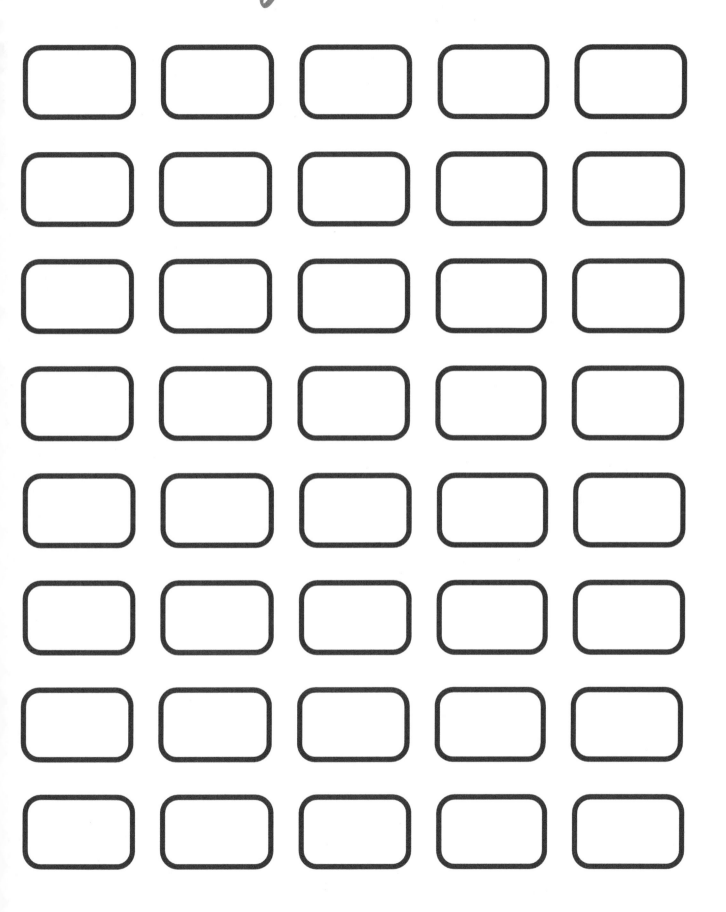

Raccoon
in Daisies

Clever, Playful, Adaptable

Mongoose

Courage, Tenacity

Ferret
in Foxgloves

Social, Curious, High-Energy

Pine Marten
in Lilies of the Valley

Cunning, Stealth

Fennec Fox
in Roses

Playful, Independent

Rabbit
in Bluebells

Fertility, Abundance, Springtime

Bunny
in Chamomile & Peony

Fertility, Abundance, Springtime

Baby Bunny
in Dandelions

Fertility, Abundance, Springtime

Badger
in Wildflowers

Determination, Protective, Fearless

Dog
in Sunflowers

Loving, Faithful, Courageous

Cat
in Dhalias

Independent, Graceful, Sensitive

Toucan
in Tropical Plants

Joyous, Communicative

Meerkat
in Peony, Feverweed & Protea

Social, Vocal, Guardian

Fawn
in Gardenias

Grace, Swiftness, Sensitivity

Fox
in California Poppies

Intelligent, Cunning, Mischievous

Fox
in Poppies

Intelligent, Cunning, Mischievous

Otter
in Riverbank Wildflowers

Playful, Clever, Adaptable

Panda
in Cherry Blossoms

Gentle, Harmonious, Happy

Weasel
in Crocuses

Cunning, Adaptable

Moose
in Roses

Majestic, Resilient, Wisdom

Owl
in Lavender

Wise, Mysterious

Squirrel

Industrioius, Perseverance

Horse

Freedom, Strength, Power

Warbler
in Roses

Energetic, Positive, Vibrant

Bear
in Lilies

Strength, Courage, Solitude

Swan

Grace, Purity, Fidelity

Chameleon

Patient, Transformitive, Individualistic

Camel
in Desert Blossoms

Endurance, Resilient

Part II
Flowers, Patterns, & Dreamscapes

Test your colors

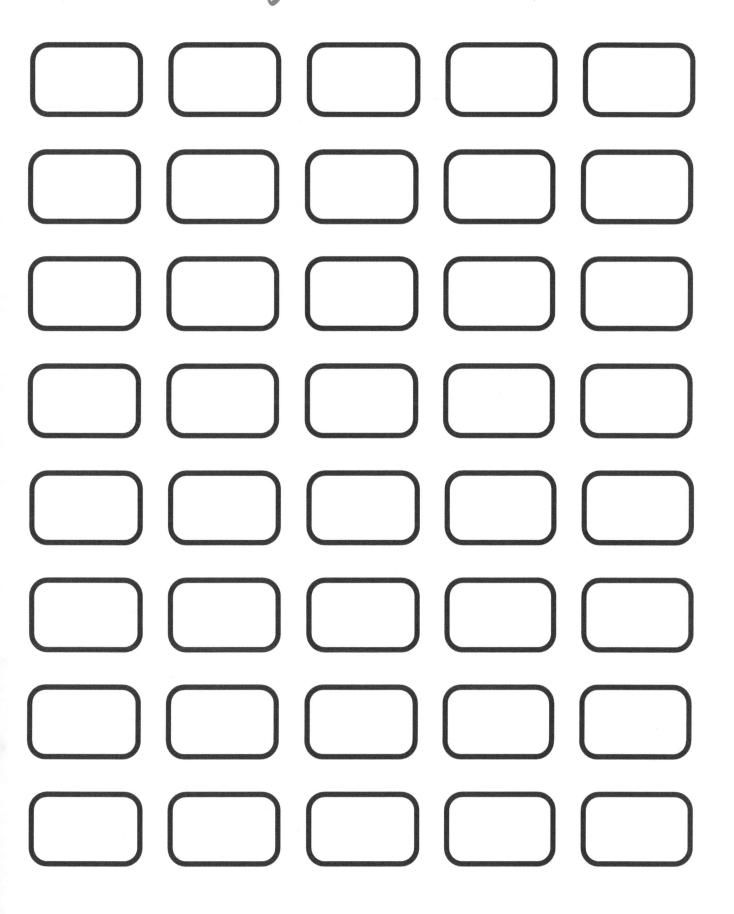

Made in United States
Cleveland, OH
07 February 2025